The Spirit of Lafayette

James Mott Hallowell

Alpha Editions

This edition published in 2024

ISBN : 9789361470608

Design and Setting By
Alpha Editions
www.alphaedis.com
Email - info@alphaedis.com

As per information held with us this book is in Public Domain.
This book is a reproduction of an important historical work. Alpha Editions uses the best technology to reproduce historical work in the same manner it was first published to preserve its original nature. Any marks or number seen are left intentionally to preserve its true form.

I

A FEW years after the signing of the Declaration of Independence a hostile Mohawk chief met in council a representative of the young American republics for the purpose of concluding a treaty of peace. The representative of young democracy was a soldier of France, the Marquis de Lafayette. Primitive America on the one hand, ancient Europe on the other! "Father," said the Indian, "we have heard thy voice and we rejoice that thou hast visited thy children to give to them good and necessary advice. Thou hast said that we have done wrong in opening our ears to wicked men, and closing our hearts to thy counsels. Father, it is all true; we have left the good path; we have wandered away from it and have been enveloped in a black cloud. We have now returned that thou mayest find in us good and faithful children. We rejoice to hear thy voice among us. It seems that the Great Spirit has directed thy footsteps to this council of friendship to smoke the calumet of peace and fellowship with thy long-lost children."

The Indian warrior's vision was true in a greater sense than he knew. Through him the soul of America spoke to the soul of Europe, and it spoke of the fellowship of man. Perhaps the footsteps of this soldier of France were indeed directed by a high Providence. Perhaps he was himself a message from the infinite. I love, for my own part, to believe that at his birth there appeared in this world an eternal and mighty spirit, a spirit perhaps from another age or sphere. Who knows? Why not? Who is there can look into the great unknown, the vast and impenetrable depths of the heavens, and say that this could not be, and was not so? How else explain this child of a French monarchy, brought up among the titled nobility of France, who amidst such conditions grew to manhood—the devotee of freedom and the ever-loyal champion of democracy?

Lafayette was born on September 6, 1757, at the Château de Chavagnac in the province of Auvergne in the monarchy of France. Two months before his birth his father was killed in battle. Left to the sole guidance of an indulgent mother, surrounded by flattering attendants and the enervating influences of wealth and noble birth, he faced the empty and useless life of a mere titled, wealthy aristocrat. What saved him? To add to these inauspicious beginnings, he was, at the age of twelve, sent to Paris to the College du Plessis where his rank and wealth introduced him to all the gaieties and dissipations of exclusive fashionable Parisian society. His mother died when he was but thirteen, leaving him in the full possession of large and valuable estates, the absolute master of his own destiny, and subject to the indulgences and corruptions of one of the most notorious courts of all Europe. Of a winning personality, he was appointed one of the

King's pages, a position much coveted by the princes and nobles of the kingdom. He was also enrolled in the King's Regiment of Mousquetaires, and at the age of fifteen through the favour of the Queen obtained a commission, an honour conferred as a mark of especial royal regard. He was married at the age of sixteen, and his young wife was a daughter of the aristocratic house of Noailles, one of the most powerful and influential families of the French court. What more profoundly barren soil could be chosen to produce the self-denying fighter for liberty, the clean-minded democrat, Lafayette?

A significant incident is told of his early life. Shortly after his marriage, his wife's family sought for him an honorary position in the household of the Count de Provençe, afterward Louis XVIII King of France. Lafayette did not wish the appointment. The spirit of Lafayette, the democrat, was already restive under royal authority. To prevent the honour being thrust upon him, and in order at the same time not to offend his family by refusing to accept, he sought an opportunity to make himself so obnoxious to the Count that the arrangement could not go through. The chance offered itself at a masked ball where the Count appeared in a disguise which was instantly penetrated by Lafayette. Making himself known, he lost no time in engaging in conversation the royal personage, who thought himself unknown, and with a freedom and boldness bordering upon discourtesy, he gave voice to facts and opinions which he knew would be obnoxious to his listener's ear. The future King of France had little hesitation in making up his mind that the young Marquis would be a refractory attaché, and declined to make the requested appointment.

Providence, or his own spirit, had saved Lafayette for democracy.

II

IN 1775 in the new western hemisphere democracy was born to the modern world.

"By the rude bridge that arched the flood,
Their flag to April's breeze unfurled,
Here once the embattled farmers stood
And fired the shot heard 'round the world."

Across the vast Atlantic rolled its echoes. Across a trackless sea, across the lands of France, up through the great White Ways of Paris it resounded. It knocked against the palace doors of the King of France. On through the flippant gibe, the careless laugh, the carousing and the din of the royal court, it reached and touched the spirit of Lafayette.

What was the strange tale that came to him from the New World? Was it a tale of liberty triumphant and conquering, a tale of success, a tale to touch the imagination of a soldier through the glory of a winning cause? Far from it. After a brief temporary success in Massachusetts the cause of the newly-born confederated American republics seemed to be tottering upon the brink of total destruction. The rout of the Americans at Brooklyn and the consequent abandonment of Long Island was followed by their evacuation of New York City. The American army was becoming demoralized. The militia were impatient to return home, were disobedient to orders, and were deserting in large numbers—it is said "by half and even by whole regiments." Then followed the Americans' defeat at White Plains, the surrender of Fort Washington, the evacuation of Fort Lee, and the steady disheartening of the American forces. The ineffectual attempts to increase the militia, the indisposition of the inhabitants to farther resistance, the retreat of General Washington through New Jersey at the head of less than three thousand men, poorly armed, almost without tents, blankets, or provisions, discouraged by constant reverses, many of them half-clad and barefooted in the cold of November and December, passing through a desponding country and pursued by a numerous, well-appointed, and victorious army—all these events made liberty at this time indeed

"A wretched soul bruised with adversity."

It was at this stage of the conflict that Lafayette determined to cross the Atlantic and take up the cause of the thirteen little republics. Benjamin Franklin, one of America's two representatives in France, who at first had welcomed this offer of assistance, upon learning of the continued American reverses, and almost despairing of the success of the cause, is reported honourably to have endeavoured to dissuade the Marquis from carrying his design into execution. Franklin and Silas Deane, the other American representative in France, told him they were unable to obtain a vessel for his passage. France was then at peace, and the King of France forbade his departure. Under the laws of France he risked the confiscation of all his property, as well as capture on the high seas. There was no winning cause to lure him, merely thirteen little newly-born republics struggling for a principle, fighting for democracy—a weak, bedraggled, and dispirited democracy, a democracy half-clad and poverty stricken, a barefooted, half-naked democracy that was very nearly down and out.

"Now," he replied to Franklin and Deane, "is precisely the moment to serve your cause; the more people are discouraged, the greater utility will result from my departure; and if you cannot furnish me with a vessel, I shall charter one at my own expense to convey your despatches and my person to the shores of America."

In a Paris paper of that year, there appears the following item:

Paris, April 4, 1777.

One of the richest of our young nobility, the Marquis de Lafayette, a relation of the Duke de Noailles, between nineteen and twenty years of age, has at his own expense hired a vessel and provided everything necessary for a voyage to America, with two officers of his acquaintance. He set out last week, having told his lady and family that he was going to Italy. He is to serve as Major-General in the American army.

III

LAFAYETTE arrived in America in June, 1777, and at once plunged into the struggle. He refused an active command at first, preferring to serve in a more humble capacity until accustomed to American troops. In the Battle of Brandywine, only some forty days after his arrival, he received a wound from a musket ball—a wound sufficient to keep him in bed for six weeks. This battle was a defeat for the American forces and was followed by the fall of the City of Philadelphia. Wounds and defeat seem, however, to have acted only as a stimulus, and in December, 1777, as a reward for intrepid and brilliant service, he was given the command of a division of the American army. He was then twenty years of age.

Then followed four years of active service under General Washington, broken only by a temporary return to France in 1779 on a diplomatic mission. Gentle and courteous, yet apparently insensible to fear, his spirit was an inspiration. At the Battle of Monmouth the enemy, during a lull, observed a general officer in the service of the Americans advancing into the danger zone, with some other officers and men, to reconnoitre the enemy's position. An aide-de-camp fell, struck by a ball, and all but the general fled precipitately. They saw the latter, although under the fire of a battery, lean to assist the stricken aide, and finding that all was ended turn and slowly rejoin the others. The British commander, General Clinton, ordered his men not to fire; and the chivalry of this Englishman probably saved the American officer's life. It was Lafayette.

In 1780 he asked leave to take a position in the Southern Department where the situation of the American army is described in a letter to Lafayette by General Greene, then commanding the division.

"It is now within a few days of the time when you shall be with me. Were you to arrive you would find a few ragged, half-starved troops in the wilderness, destitute of everything necessary for either the comfort or convenience of soldiers.... The country is almost laid waste and the inhabitants plunder one another with little less than savage fury. We live from hand to mouth, and have nothing to subsist on but what we collect with armed parties.... I fear this department is to be the great Serbonian bog to the American armies and particularly to the general officers."

The vision of a Serbonian bog acted only as a magnet, and Lafayette started to join Greene. On his way, however, he was recalled by the commander-in-chief, General Washington, to take command of an expedition against Benedict Arnold, the traitor, now a brigadier-general in the enemy's army, who was marching into Virginia and with revengeful fury carrying fire and sword wherever he went. Lafayette was dispatched against him with specific orders that if Arnold surrendered there should be no stipulation made for his safety, and at the same time forbidding the slightest injury to his person;—it being the purpose of Washington, never however fulfilled, to bring Arnold to public punishment according to the rules and regulations of the army.

Lafayette's command seems to have been no better than Greene's. In a letter to Greene he describes his men as being in a condition of "shocking nakedness." Even the officers were destitute of money, clothing, and everything that could contribute to cleanliness and comfort. As for the men, they were poorly fed, their shoes worn out, without tents, and destitute of almost any protection from the inclemency of the weather. Some of his officers assured the Marquis that his command would speedily be reduced one-half by desertion,—and as a matter of fact thirteen out of one company deserted in a single day. A nauseous and contagious disease, generally produced by a want of cleanliness, overspread nearly the entire command. In consequence of these difficulties, Arnold escaped, but Lafayette forced his retreat.

The military genius of George Washington at last turned the tide of war. In October, 1781, he had the enemy's troops under Cornwallis cornered at Yorktown. In the course of the siege it became necessary to capture a certain redoubt possessed by the enemy. Washington determined to carry it with the bayonet, and appointed Lafayette to conduct the charge. The American infantry advanced with irresistible power, relying entirely upon their bayonets, and carried the redoubt by assault.

Shortly afterward Cornwallis surrendered his entire army to Washington, and the last battle of the American Revolution had been fought. In November, 1781, the confederated republics having won, Lafayette returned to France.

Washington and Lafayette! The American and the Frenchman. Great soldiers both, but above all, great *men*. The real soul of the soldier speaks out in this letter from the American to the Frenchman, written in 1784: "At length, my dear Marquis, I have become a private citizen on the banks of the Potomac; and under the shadow of my own vine and my own fig-tree, free from the bustle of the camp and the busy scenes of public life, I am solacing myself with those tranquil enjoyments, of which the soldier who is ever in pursuit of fame, the statesman whose watchful days and sleepless nights are spent in devising schemes to promote the welfare of his own, perhaps the ruin of other countries, as if this globe was insufficient for us all—and the courtier who is always watching the countenance of his prince in the hope of catching a gracious smile—can have very little conception. I have not only retired from all public employments, but am retiring within myself and shall be able to view the solitary walk, and tread the paths of private life with heartfelt satisfaction. Envious of none, I am determined to be pleased with all; and this, my dear friend, being the order of my march, I shall move gently down the stream of life until I sleep with my fathers."

IV

THE scene in the world-wide drama of democracy shifts across the Atlantic Ocean, from America to France. The French Revolution of 1789 and the Reign of Terror—a century's pent-up rage against despotism, let loose in a single hour!

When Madame Roland was summoned before the revolutionary tribunal she came with a smile upon her lips, her face sparkling with life and animation. Condemned in advance, she was falsely declared guilty of being the author of a "mutinous conspiracy against the unity and defense of the republic." She heard her sentence calmly. "You deem me worthy the fate of the great men you have murdered. I shall try to display the same courage on the scaffold." She was at once taken in a cart to the Place de la Revolution, a man guilty of treason being placed in the same cart. He was overwhelmed with terror and she occupied her time in soothing him. On reaching the guillotine, she bade him mount the steps first, that his sufferings might not be prolonged. As she took her place, her eyes fell on a colossal statue of Liberty, recently erected near by. "O Liberty," she cried, "what crimes are committed in thy name!"

"There is no God." Thus in 1793, by solemn enactment of the Terrorists, was the Deity legislated out of existence. There is no God! What sayest thou now, Robespierre? Dost thou say so, *now*? How likedst thou thy brief space of usurpation? A few brief months of power—night and day with loaded pistols at thy side—no food till some one else had tasted from thy dish, lest it be poisoned. And then another scene in that same legislative hall, the hall of thy own great terrifying power. A vote ordering thy arrest! Vain are thy shrieks—a detachment of thy own soldiers forces its way into the room—a pistol shot rings out, and thou with shattered jaw, a ghastly spectacle, facest thy end. Thou fallest, and some spit upon thy prostrate form, others stab thee with their knives. Still living, thy body is hurried before the tribunal thou thyself didst form, and thence to the guillotine. O Robespierre, thinkest thou now there is a God?

License, not liberty. Mania, not reason. How fared the spirit of Lafayette during this debauchery in the name of freedom?

V

A BRIEF interval of less than ten years intervened between the closing scenes of the American Revolution and the opening scenes of the French Revolution. Democracy in America was a victor, and the republic had been established. Democracy in France was just entering upon its cyclonic and hideous struggle for the right to live.

The government of France was at that time an absolute despotism. The king was the supreme arbiter of its destinies. He was the head of the army. He appointed his own ministers, made his own laws, levied and raised taxes at his pleasure, and lavished his treasures as he pleased. The common people were more like cattle than men. They tilled the ground and bore the yoke; the king and the aristocracy wielded the whip. Years of suffering ignorance for the many—years of riotous profligacy for the few!

True democracy is world-wide. It knows no nationality. All mankind are its countrymen. When at the close of the American war Lafayette returned to France, he hung in his house a copy of the American Declaration of Independence upon one of the walls, leaving the corresponding space on the opposite side vacant. "What do you mean to place here?" asked one of his friends. "A Declaration of Rights for France," he replied.

Frederick the Great, King of Prussia, the first giant of the Hohenzollerns and the fountain head of modern Prussian autocracy, attracted by Lafayette's military reputation, invited him to the royal palace at Potsdam to witness and take part in the review of the Prussian army. At dinner one evening Frederick declared confidently his opinion that America would not long be a republic, but would return to the good old system. "Never, sir," replied his guest. "A monarchy, a nobility can never exist in America." "Sir," said the monarch, "I knew a young man who, after having visited countries where liberty and equality reigned, conceived the idea of establishing the same system in his own country. Do you know what happened to him?" "No, sir." "He was hanged," replied the King with a smile.

In 1789 the mutterings of the coming storm became more ominous, but the King of France, deafened by the clamour of cackling advice from his aristocracy, either could not or would not hear. Almost bankrupt because of the extravagance of the court, he needed money, still more money, and called an "assembly of notables" to assist in devising measures to relieve his embarrassed finances. They were men from the most distinguished of the nobility. Lafayette was one. In a letter to Washington he humorously remarked that "wicked people called them not-ables." Lafayette's part in the assembly consisted in making a bold protest against the prodigality of the crown. "All the millions given up to cupidity or depredation," he forcefully exclaimed to the noble gathering, "are the fruit of the sweat, the tears, and perhaps the blood, of the nation"; and he concluded by requesting that the King convoke a real National Assembly, made up of representatives of the common people. It was the beginning of the Revolution. For Lafayette's part in this the King's prime minister, Calonne, proposed to the monarch to send Lafayette to the Bastile.

Nothing was accomplished by the notables, and the monarch then decided to assemble the states-general. This was not a legislative body, but an assembly of representatives from the nobility, the clergy, and the common people, sometimes called by the crown when it needed assistance, the commons always being in the minority. The commons, *le tiers état* grasped the opportunity, met by themselves, and on June 17, 1789, resolved themselves into a National Assembly, to accomplish the regeneration of France.

Troops were summoned by the crown to put down the rebellion, and more than fifty thousand mercenary troops from foreign states were engaged by the King to take the place of the French troops, whom he distrusted. Lafayette joined with the National Assembly, and then and there proposed to it the first draft of that French Declaration of Rights for which he had prophetically left a space on the wall of his home. The essence of his draft lies in the following extract: "No man can be subject to any laws, excepting those which have received the assent of himself or his representatives, and which are promulgated beforehand and applied legally. The principle of all sovereignty resides in the nation."

On July 14, 1789, the storm broke. The gigantic fortress of the Bastile which for ages had reared its menacing head among the people of Paris, a terrible engine of despotic military autocracy, was attacked and taken by the mob. M. De Launay, its Governor, was killed by a bayonet thrust, and his head cut from his body and carried through the streets upon a pitchfork. "And in this bloody manner, into those dungeons where thousands had wasted away, often without trial and with no knowledge of the charges against them, liberty sent her first ray of sunlight."

"When oppression renders a revolution necessary, insurrection becomes the holiest of duties," was the ringing message of Lafayette to the Assembly. The key of the Bastile was given to him as the representative of freedom in Europe, and together with a sketch of the ruins of that fortress of despotism, he sent it to George Washington. "It is a tribute," he wrote, "which I owe, as a son to my adopted father—as an aide-de-camp to my general—as a missionary of liberty to its patriarch."

A National Guard, a new army of two hundred thousand citizen soldiers, was authorized and formed by the National Assembly, both for the protection of the rights of the people at home and for resistance to possible foreign aggression. Lafayette, now thirty-two years of age, was chosen its commander-in-chief. Thus was born democracy in France.

VI

A FOREIGN peasant, from a land of despotic autocracy, who had just immigrated to the United States, was once haled into one of our police courts, charged with almost murdering his wife with a club. His defense was that he now was in a land of liberty and he thought he could do what he liked. Multiply this by a million-fold and you have the Reign of Terror, the second chapter of the French Revolution.

"*Aimez les amis du peuple et l'enthousiasme pour la liberté, mais réservez l'aveugle soumission pour la loi,*" said Lafayette to the Federation of National Guards. The atrocities, both at the storming of the Bastile and afterward, he would not countenance, and on more than one occasion, at the head of his armed troops, he enforced law and order. Finally, Austria and Prussia declared war upon France, and Lafayette was sent from Paris and at the head of a French army of twenty-eight thousand men was stationed at Sedan.

It was inevitable that he and the Jacobins, the leaders in the mad orgy of debauched democracy that succeeded the initial stages of the revolution, should soon split. For a long time the Jacobins had seemed to shrink from a contest with him, probably because they hoped to win him over to their excesses. Finding him inflexible, when at last they controlled the government, they vowed his destruction, and he was deprived of his command. They proposed that a price should be set upon his head and that "*chaque citoyen pût courir sus*"—that is to say, that any one who pleased might murder him.

Deprived of his command, and with destruction awaiting him in the rear, his only resource was flight. Even then he hesitated, but reason prevailed and on a dark and rainy night, with a few companions on horseback, he started for Holland. To get there he had to pass through territory occupied by the Austrian and Prussian troops. Facing the almost certain chance of falling in with a superior force, he determined to make a bold front, and went directly to the Austrian commander at Namur, declaring that he was a French officer attached to constitutional measures and seeking an asylum in Holland. Instead of being given a passport, he was, when recognized, detained, given over to a Prussian commander, sent in a cart to Wesel on the Rhine and there put in a cell in irons. It was then intimated to him that the burden of the situation would be lightened if he would draw up certain plans to be used against France. The Prussians, finding that he would not do this, instead of treating him as a prisoner of war threw him into a dungeon at Magdebourg. His estate at home was confiscated and his wife imprisoned. After a year's imprisonment at Magdebourg in a dirty and humid vault he was transferred by the Prussians from one dungeon to another, and at last confined in the Austrian citadel of Olmutz.

The walls of his dungeon at Olmutz were six feet thick and the air was admitted through openings two feet square secured at each end by massive iron bars. Before these loopholes was situated a broad ditch, which was filled with water only when it rained; at other times it was a stagnant marsh continually emitting disease; beyond this were the outer walls of the castle, so that the slightest breeze could never refresh the inmate. Each cell had two doors, one of iron, the other of wood nearly two feet thick, and both were covered with bolts, bars, and padlocks. When the soldiers twice a day brought the prisoner's wretched portion it was carefully examined to find out if there was any note or communication contained in it. A messy bed of rotten straw filled with vermin, together with a broken chair and an old worm-eaten table, formed the whole furniture of his establishment. The cell was from eight to ten paces long and six wide; in storms the water frequently flowed through the loopholes; when the sun did not shine he remained almost in darkness during the whole day.

He was a prisoner of war and entitled to be treated as such. But instead he was confined in a dungeon and was given to believe that he would never again see beyond its four walls, that he would never receive news of any events or persons, that his name would be unknown in the citadel, and that in all accounts of him sent to Court he would be designated only by a number. Even knives and forks were denied him, and he was told that this was done because his situation was such as naturally to lead to suicide. His sufferings proved almost beyond his strength. The want of air and decent food, and the loathsome dampness of his dungeon brought him more than once to the borders of the grave. His frame was wasted by diseases, and on one occasion he was so reduced that "his hair fell from him entirely by the excess of his sufferings."

Following a bold attempt to escape, the torture of his imprisonment was increased. Irons were securely fastened around his ankles. During the winter of 1794-1795, which was extremely severe, he had a violent fever and almost died; he was deprived of proper attendance, of air, of suitable food, and of decent clothes; in this state he had nothing for his bed but a little damp and mouldy straw; around his waist was a chain which was fastened to the wall and barely permitted him to turn from one side to the other. No light was admitted into his cell. To increase his miseries, almost insupportable mental anguish was added to his physical suffering. He was made to believe that he was only saved for a public execution, while at the same time he was not permitted to know whether his family were still alive or had perished under the axe during the Reign of Terror.

A Prussian statesman to whom in 1793 a memorial had been addressed soliciting Lafayette's release is said to have replied: "Lafayette has too much fanaticism for liberty. He does not conceal it. All his letters prove it. If he were out of prison he could not remain quiet. I saw him when he was here and I shall always recollect one of his expressions, which surprised me very much at the time: 'Do you believe,' said he, 'that I went to America to obtain military reputation?—it was for liberty I went there. He who loves liberty can only remain quiet after having established it in his own country.'"

O liberty, hard is thy path! License wearing thy mask at home, and thy champion betrayed to the dungeon of thy eternal foe!

VII

OUT of the chaos rose the dictator. Napoleon's comet was beginning to ascend.

Napoleon Bonaparte in 1797 was commander in Italy of the victorious army of the French Republic, and as such he demanded of Austria that the French prisoners in the fortress of Olmutz be set at liberty. Consent was given as to the others, but only after much talk and grudgingly as to Lafayette. His unconquerable hostility to the reigning autocracies was too well known, and Austria even attempted to impose the terms that, if freed, Lafayette should be deported to America under promise never again to put his foot either in Austria or Prussia. But Lafayette himself would not consent to be freed on these terms, and Napoleon insisted; so, finally, at the dictation of Napoleon Bonaparte, on September 19, 1797, after more than five years' imprisonment, Lafayette's fetters were knocked off and he was released. Napoleon afterward often alluded to the intense hatred of the monarchs and royal cabinets of Europe for the democrat Lafayette. "I am sufficiently hated," said he one day to Lafayette, "by the princes and their courtiers; but it is nothing to their hatred for you. I have been so situated as to see it, and I could not have believed that human hate could go so far."

Perhaps at no time was the spirit of Lafayette put to a greater test than in the years that followed—the years of the rise of imperial Napoleon, Emperor of the French.

Revenge against his prison keepers, the certainty of high success, the excitement of a great popular cause, military glory, gratitude to his deliverer, all coördinated to make him follow the path of conquest, and lead with Napoleon. He could have been one of the great military heroes of those times. But apparently these temptations rebounded from him as an arrow from a steel plate. When only a boy of seventeen, his noble relatives had been unable to conceive his refusing an honorable place in royalty's household. It had been inconceivable to the Prussian that this Frenchman had not gone to America on a quest solely for military glory. The Jacobin clubs, first by fair promises and then by the demand for his life blood, had sought to force him from liberty to license, from real freedom to debauched freedom. But like Sir Galahad, the Knight of the Holy Grail, he had stood true to his quest, true to his ideal, true to the inward light that unerringly marked the real from the false, true to genuine democracy in its fight against autocracy. And now, greater than all these lures and tests, stood before him Napoleon Bonaparte, his deliverer, the greatest military captain of the world beckoning him to paths of fame. The sceptre of all that the professional soldier held dear was thrust into his hands. He could not be false unto himself, and the sceptre was turned aside.

When he found that Napoleon was plotting against the democracy of France, that a new imperial power was rising in Napoleon's person, he deliberately broke off his relations with the general. During the days of the French conquests under Napoleon he lived the life of a quiet country gentleman, interested solely in domestic life, agriculture, and the pursuit of reading and science. The man who had staked his all in a desperate chance in the war of democracy against despotic autocracy would not raise his finger in a war of conquest for the aggrandizement of an emperor, though driven by the demon of revenge, drawn by the ties of gratitude, and enticed by the lure of glory.

VIII

ON MARCH 1, 1815, Napoleon returned from Elba and began the final act in the great drama of his life. In a last effort to win Lafayette to his side, he sent his brother Joseph Bonaparte on a special mission to Lafayette with word that the latter's name was placed first upon Napoleon's list of peers. Joseph returned with a refusal. "Should I ever again appear upon the sea of public life," Lafayette had replied, "it will only be as a representative of the people."

Waterloo!—and Napoleon disappeared forever from the world drama. Then came back the Bourbons, first Louis XVIII, followed by Charles X. Step by step, under the Bourbon *régime*, autocracy began to regain its grip upon France. The year 1830 opened ominously. The rumblings of 1789 were again heard. The French Chamber of Deputies protested against the growing usurpations of the crown. The King boldly defied them, dissolved the Chamber, annulled the electoral laws then in force, reduced the number of deputies nearly one-half, and materially changed the conditions of suffrage and representation.

Lafayette was at his country estate, La Grange, when the *Moniteur* with a copy of these decrees reached him. He immediately set out for Paris. Revolt had already commenced, and war was raging in the streets of the city. The revolutionists wanted a leader and all eyes turned to Lafayette. He was called by acclamation to command the National Guard.

He was now seventy-two years of age, but he accepted the call. Immediately he established his headquarters in Paris and passed the whole night inspecting barriers and preparing for a renewal of the battle on the morrow. At dawn it began again and the National Guard under Lafayette drove back the royal troops and carried all before them. On July 29, 1830, the Chamber of Deputies reassembled, organized a provisional government, and formally invested Lafayette with the powers of military dictator of France. "Liberty shall triumph," he replied in his letter of acceptance, "or we will perish together."

Charles X, seeing the hopelessness of the royal cause, sent a deputation to Lafayette to announce the revocation of the obnoxious decrees and the nomination of a new and liberal ministry. "It is too late," Lafayette sent word back, "all conciliation is impossible. The royal family has ceased to reign." Thus ended the dynasty of the elder branch of the Bourbons on the throne of France. The deposed king was allowed to pass unmolested to another country.

The people who had accomplished the revolution, especially the citizen army, loudly demanded a republic with Lafayette for its president. Others begged him to mount the throne himself. But to all these entreaties he turned a deaf ear. He thought not of himself but of France alone.

A constitutional monarchy, under Louis Phillippe, followed. It was successful at first, until the old, old story of attempted autocratic usurpation was again repeated by the monarch. He was forcibly ejected, and the Republic of 1848 was formed. But long ere this, moving gently down the stream of life, the journey had ended, and Lafayette slept with his fathers. *Vive l'ésprit de Lafayette!*

"The stars shall fade away, the sun himself
Grow dim with age, and nature sink in years,
But thou shalt flourish in immortal youth,
Unhurt amidst the war of elements,
The wrecks of matter, and the crush of worlds."

IX

EVERY person has two selves, the shell and the real self beneath. Acts are the evidence of the real self. Let us hope what is best in the real self is eternal, for thus only does the world progress.

Lafayette symbolized two great principles of government. First, the right of a people to govern themselves, as opposed to government of the many by a self-appointed few—in other words, democracy as opposed to autocracy. Second, a union of the democracies to insure mutual protection and peace.

When only a boy at school, he was told in class one day to describe a perfect courser, and he sacrificed his hope of obtaining a premium by describing a horse which on perceiving the whip threw down his master. He adopted on his arms the device, "*Cur non?*"—"Why not?" Before landing in America in 1777 he wrote to his wife: "I but offer my services to that interesting republic from motives of the purest kind, unmixed with ambition or private views: her happiness and my glory are my only incentives to the task. I hope that, for my sake, you will be a good American, for that feeling is worthy of every noble heart. The happiness of America is intimately connected with the happiness of all mankind; she will become the safe and respected asylum of virtue, integrity, toleration, equality, and tranquil happiness."

In camp at Valley Forge, January, 1778, he writes to his wife, who was then seeking his return: "The desire ... to promote ... the happiness of humanity which is strongly interested in the existence of one perfectly free nation ... forbids my departure."

Upon a return visit to America in 1784, speaking to a deputation from the Pennsylvania Legislature, he said: "Now that the great work is accomplished let us mutually congratulate ourselves on the federal union which this peace has cemented, and upon which the importance, the power, and the riches of this beautiful country rest; that union is the bond which will continue to preserve brotherly love and reciprocal friendship among the citizens of the states. I shall be happy to receive the command of this Republic at every period of my existence and in whatever part of the world I may be; my zeal for its prosperity is only equalled by my gratitude and respect." A statement from his reply to a special committee appointed by Congress to wait upon him shows the same feeling: "May this immense temple of freedom ever stand a lesson to oppressors, an example to the oppressed, and a sanctuary for the rights of mankind."

The confederation in 1776 of the thirteen separate colonies of the western world was a union of all the then existing democracies of a hemisphere, to insure mutual protection and peace. Since then, democracy has been born in the Old World. In its common cause it knows no nationality. Lafayette is the symbol of its internationalism. In the time of our greatest stress he crossed the ocean to us, saying: "Now is precisely the moment to serve your cause." To-day democracy in France is bleeding to death. Throughout Europe, assailed in front by the giant of Prussian militarism and stabbed in the back by assassins conducting an insidious and treacherous peace propaganda, it is staggering under the combined attack. The spirit of Lafayette, the democrat, calls to us across that same ocean. The bugles of the heavens ring out. The days of '76 are born again. Once more is heard the battle-cry of the Republic. Where his spirit calls, our armies go. And when the great work is accomplished, we shall cement the union which he began.

X

BUT is democracy worth preserving? How fares that intangible something which was the inspiration of this man's living? Democracy, the right of people to govern themselves, as opposed to their control by a self-appointed few—is it a failure or a success? Has it proved itself worth the dedication of this soldier spirit?

The French, for themselves, have answered the question at the Battle of the Marne and at Verdun. But how about America? Has the great American democracy proved a success, as compared with government by autocracy—for example, as compared with the government of Germany by the Prussian military autocracy, headed by the House of Hohenzollern?

More than a century has passed since the surrender of Cornwallis. Since then in physical growth and material success the democracy of the United States has more than fulfilled the highest hopes. At that time these United States were only a strip along the eastern seaboard, bounded on the east by the Atlantic Ocean and on the west by an unexplored wilderness; thirteen sparsely settled states, the settlements widely separated from each other, with a population of less than four million persons. Now the wilderness is overcome. By the Louisiana Purchase we acquired the Great Southwest. For a pittance we bought the wastes of Alaska and then found them to be the gold fields of the world. The Philippines, with an area of one hundred and fifteen thousand square miles, and the Hawaiian Islands mark the extension of our western boundaries. Cuba is under our immediate protection. Porto Rico is part of us, and likewise the Danish West Indies. In Central America we have built the Panama Canal. By the Monroe Doctrine we are the protectors from foreign interference of all of Central and South America. Our population has grown to more than one hundred million souls. Our material wealth is the greatest of any single nation in the world.

Does this constitute success? Look on the other side of the picture. Our form of national government has been notoriously inefficient—taking Germany as the standard. Our state governments at their best are mediocre, while at their worst they stand pitifully paralyzed before mob law. Our unpunished lynchings of coloured people, innocent as well as guilty, make us contemptible in the eyes of the civilized world. No other government on earth remains silent and helpless while its citizens assemble as for a holiday and burn a criminal at the stake. Our municipalities are largely rotten with graft, and the graft is accompanied by its inevitable handmaids, extravagance and inefficiency. Enormous wealth, in the hands of a few, dwells side by side with extreme poverty. Our cities are overcrowded, and the country of Whittier, where

"Shut in from all the world without
We sat the clean-winged hearth about,"

is handed over to the huts and shanties of immigrants. Capital fights labour and labour fights capital. Politics are such that most men avoid them. The standard of work is not how well you can do your job, but how much you can make out of it. Is this democracy a success?

In answer to this, however, does not an inner consciousness in each of us, perhaps the spirit of Lafayette and perhaps our own, perhaps the whispering of an unseen, great, and infinite power, tell us that the really relevant question is not whether we have yet achieved success, but whether a successful democracy is worth striving for? If, however, I should be obliged to answer the question by "Yes" or "No" I would say, "Yes, it is a success!"

The best route for the development of any man lies along the hard and thorny road of self-development. In the end, self-development, by dint of hard work and mistakes, produces the best man, provided he has the courage to "see it through." Nations are merely big collections of individuals. In the end this self-development produces the best nation. The road is filled with difficulties, but so are most roads to goals that are worth reaching.

Our national government may have been inefficient in its details, but taken as a whole it has created a country which for generations has been a haven for the oppressed of the world. How many hundred thousand Germans have immigrated to America? How many Americans have ever emigrated to Germany? We have lynchings in the South, but no other country was ever left a more hideous problem of slavery, and in 1861 when the supreme test came the government rose to it; no one but a visionary can expect an immediate Utopian readjustment. Our municipalities abound in graft, but what country before ours ever faced the problem of absorbing annually the enormous flood of unlettered immigrants that is unceasingly poured upon us by the Old World. The wonder is not that we have graft, but that we have not more graft. We have great wealth and extreme poverty, but they are due to unusual economic causes, namely: great national resources on the one hand, and ceaseless immigration on the other. Our cities are overcrowded and our standards of work are superficial, but would this be cured by a despotism?

And always we have the hope that goes with liberty, the undying strength that accompanies the knowledge that you are master of your own soul. A good despot at the head of a military autocracy may for the time being make the most efficient government in the world; certainly a bad despot at the head of a military autocracy makes the worst government. But I will never believe that the total surrender of the individual to the guiding hand of a despotic autocracy makes in the end for the progress of the whole. History shows it to be untrue; the never-ceasing efforts of democracy, as endless as the waves of the sea, show that despotic autocracy cannot last; and the hell let loose upon earth by Prussian autocracy, its modern exponent, clinches the falsity of its creed for all but the intoxicated or maniacs.

XI

NOW has arisen the Menace, the eternal foe of a free people, the Prussian Creed. The following is a composite statement of Prussianism: "compiled sentence by sentence from the utterances of Prussians, the Kaiser and his generals, professors, editors, and Nietzsche, part of it said in cold blood, years before this war, and all of it a declaration of faith now being ratified by action." It is taken word for word from the eleventh chapter of Owen Wister's remarkable work "The Pentecost of Calamity,"[A] and is the most concise statement of the Menace that I have seen.

[A] "The Pentecost of Calamity," by Owen Wister. The Macmillan Company.

"We Hohenzollerns take our crown from God alone. On me the Spirit of God has descended. I regard my whole ... task as appointed by heaven. Who opposes me I shall crush to pieces. Nothing must be settled in this world without the intervention ... of ... the German Emperor. He who listens to public opinion runs a danger of inflicting immense harm on ... the State. When one occupies certain positions in the world one ought to make dupes rather than friends. Christian morality cannot be political. Treaties are only a disguise to conceal other political aims. Remember that the German people are the chosen of God.

"Might is right and ... is decided by war. Every youth who enters a beer-drinking and duelling club will receive the true direction of his life. War in itself is a good thing. God will see to it that war always recurs. The efforts directed toward the abolition of war must not only be termed foolish, but absolutely immoral. The peace of Europe is only a secondary matter for us. The sight of suffering does one good; the infliction of suffering does one more good. This war must be conducted as ruthlessly as possible.

"The Belgians should not be shot *dead*. They should be ... so left as to make impossible all hope of recovery. The troops are to treat the Belgian civil population with unrelenting severity and frightfulness. Weak nations have not the same right to live as powerful ... nations. The world has no longer need of little nationalities. We Germans have little esteem and less respect ... for Holland. We need to enlarge our colonial possessions; such territorial acquisitions we can only realize at the cost of other states.

"Russia must no longer be our frontier. The Polish press should be annihilated ... likewise the French and Danish.... The Poles should be allowed ... three privileges: to pay taxes, serve in the army, and shut their jaws. France must be so completely crushed that she will never again cross our path. You must remember that we have not come to make war on the French people, but to bring them the higher Civilization. The French have shown themselves decadent and without respect for the Divine law. Against England we fight for booty. Our real enemy is England. We have to ... crush absolutely perfidious Albion ... subdue her to such an extent that her influence all over the world is broken forever.

"German should replace English as the world language. English, the bastard tongue ... must be swept into the remotest corners ... until it has returned to its original elements of an insignificant pirate dialect. The German language acts as a blessing which, coming direct from the hand of God, sinks into the heart like a precious balm. To us, more than any other nation, is intrusted the true structure of human existence. Our own country, by employing military power, has attained a degree of Culture which it could never have reached by peaceful means.

"The civilization of mankind suffers every time a German becomes an American. Let us drop our miserable attempts to excuse Germany's action. We willed it. Our might shall create a new law in Europe. It is Germany that strikes. We are morally and intellectually superior beyond all comparison.... We must ... fight with Russian beasts, English mercenaries, and Belgian fanatics. We have nothing to apologize for. It is no consequence whatever if all the monuments ever created, all the pictures ever painted, all the buildings ever erected by the great architects of the world, be destroyed.... The ugliest stone placed to mark the burial of a German grenadier is a more glorious monument than all the cathedrals of Europe put together. No respect for the tombs of Shakespeare, Newton, and Faraday.

"They call us barbarians. What of it? The German claim must be: ... Education to hate ... Organization of hatred ... Education to the desire for hatred. Let us abolish unripe and false shame.... To us is given faith, hope, and hatred; but hatred is the greatest among them."

The German war code, introduction, paragraph three, reads as follows: "A war conducted with energy cannot be directed merely against the combatants of the enemy state, and the positions which they occupy, but will in like manner seek to destroy the total intellectual and material resources of the latter."

XII

WE ARE at war. On April 6, 1917, the democracy of the United States of America formally declared war against the autocracy of Germany. What are we fighting for?

Two brutes in the shape of men engage in a savage, drunken brawl. Bloody, cursing, dishevelled, with swollen and distorted features, and screaming their anathemas of drunken hate, they fight with the ferocity of beasts. Beasts they are.

A bully, a degenerate, a thug of the city, a brigand of the country, a horse thief of the western plains, attacks a weaker and unprepared victim. A man with red blood in his veins sees the assault, and attacks the attacker with strength enough to save the victim, arrest the disturber of the peace, and prevent a repetition of the offense. He has been engaged in a fight, but he is not a beast.

The spirit of Lafayette brought him to America to fight for democracy; he was a hard fighter but he was not a beast. And now, against that calculating and brutal power which with the treachery of a tiger of the jungle and all the devilish ingenuity of the highest Kultur has assaulted the peace of the world, the armies of America are led by the spirit of Lafayette.

For years the Prussian military autocracy has been preparing for the leap upon its victim. The power to declare war has been kept solely and exclusively in the hands of the military autocracy. It is responsible to no one. The great mass of people must do as they are commanded; obeying, not laws made by themselves acting through their duly-elected representatives, but orders promulgated by a self-appointed few, the military autocracy of Prussia. Woe to the unfortunate victim who refuses to obey! With cold-blooded deliberation this military autocracy which controls the German people has for years been preparing its huge fighting machine. When the time to strike came, when the neighbouring countries were least prepared to resist, Germany was deluged with the lie that the German nation was attacked, the scrap of paper otherwise called a treaty was torn up, and the tiger sprang. The world knows the result.

We enter the war for two motives, one to preserve the democracies of Europe, the other for our own preservation. The sinking of our ships by submarines was merely the immediate cause, the match that lit the fire, just as the firing on Fort Sumter was the proximate but not the real cause of our Civil War. The real cause of our Civil War was, as Lincoln said, because this nation "could not endure half slave and half free." The real cause of the present World War is because civilization cannot endure half military autocracy and half free democracy. "The world must be made safe for democracy." We fight to save the intended victims of Prussianism, to arrest the disturber of the peace, and prevent a repetition of the offense.

The President of the United States in his great message, delivered in the Congress of the United States on the second day of April, 1917, in which he advised the Congress to accept the status of belligerent thrust upon us by the acts of the Imperial Government of Germany in unlawfully sinking our ships and killing our citizens, said: "Let us be very clear, and make very clear to all the world what our motives and our objects are.... Our object ... is to vindicate the principles of peace and justice in the life of the world as against selfish and autocratic power and to set up amongst the really free and self-governed peoples of the world such a concert of purpose and of action as will henceforth ensure the observance of those principles. Neutrality is no longer feasible or desirable where the peace of the world is involved and the freedom of its peoples, and the menace to that peace and freedom lies in the existence of autocratic governments backed by organized force which is controlled wholly by their will, not by the will of their people....

"We are now about to accept gauge of battle with this natural foe to liberty and shall, if necessary, spend the whole force of the nation to check and nullify its pretensions and its power.... The world must be made safe for democracy. Its peace must be planted upon the tested foundations of political liberty. We have no selfish ends to serve. We desire no conquest, no dominion. We seek no indemnities for ourselves, no material compensation for the sacrifices we shall freely make. We are but one of the champions of the rights of mankind. We shall be satisfied when those rights have been made as secure as the faith and the freedom of nations can make them."

XIII

WE ARE at war with the Menace. It is the same Menace—now grown to a monster with four heads dominated by one brain—that over a hundred years ago invited Lafayette to its palace at Potsdam to review the Prussian army, and then cynically suggested to him an end upon the scaffold. It is the same Menace, now from its four mouths spitting its spume of hate upon a chaotic world, that thrust the body of the champion of democracy into a dungeon, but could not kill his soul. Our present war against this creature of evil is but one more act in the drama begun by the spirit of Lafayette.

How shall this act end? Listen to this. I quote largely from André Chéradame, a man who deals not in platitudes and conceits to tickle the vanity of a nation, but in cold, hard facts.

In 1914, when the war began, Prussian militarism controlled Germany, with a population of sixty-eight millions; and Germany had one ally, Austria-Hungary, of whose thirty million people a majority were directly antagonistic to Berlin. By the spring of 1915 it had extended and organized its power among these thirty million Austro-Hungarians, who until that time had taken orders from their own independent military chiefs. In the fall of 1915 it joined hands with Bulgaria and Turkey over the corpse of Serbia. Thus, since the beginning of the war, has been formed the Quadruple Alliance, dominated by Prussian militarism.

This alliance, or Prussia before the alliance was completed, has since the beginning of the war seized Belgium, Poland, Serbia, Albania, Montenegro, part of France, and most of Roumania. The population now controlled by Prussian militarism is about one hundred and seventy-five million people. The economic resources controlled by it show a corresponding increase. Before the war began, Prussia planned for a Pan-Germanism of this nature, and this plan has now been almost completed.

If Prussia can now, by granting pretentious but ineffective political reforms to its own people and by fighting a defensive war until the contest becomes a deadlock, hold this Pan-Germany in its present position, then after peace has been declared it can organize this vast additional strength in man power and resources which it has gained, can Prussianize this additional one hundred million, can, by the same intrigue which it has used in the past, undermine during this period of peace the internal defensive effectiveness of the democracies, and when the time comes can strike again.

And if the democracies are unable to win now, what chance will they have then?

Drop the scales from our eyes and look clearly at the facts, hard as they are. The Menace has been fighting a winning fight. By merely keeping a deadlock for the rest of the war, and forcing a truce under the guise of peace, the Menace will win; provided, however, that it is not expelled by the German people themselves. This is the strength—and the weakness—of the foe against which we have declared war.

The Prussian looks a long way ahead. M. Chéradame, in his work, "Le Complot Pan-Germaniste Demasqué," recites the following incident: "In 1898, before Manila, the German Rear-Admiral von Goetzen, a friend of the Kaiser, said to the American Admiral Dewey, 'In about fifteen years my country will begin a great war.... Some months after we have done our business in Europe we shall take New York and probably Washington, and we shall keep them for a time.... We shall extract one or two billions of dollars from New York and other towns.'" The months referred to by the German sailor may be turned into years, and the one or two billions may be multiplied by ten—but the Prussian looks a long way ahead.

XIV

HOW can our rights and the rights of mankind to which the President has alluded be made secure? What definite concrete facts must be established in order that democracy may be made safe?

In the first place, the autocratic power that now puts terror into the heart of the world must be broken beyond repair. The Hohenzollerns and the rest of the military caste which now controls Germany must be politically exterminated. No pretended or half-way internal political reforms, leaving a road for their return to power, will be sufficient. Annihilate the Menace. The cancer must be cut out, with no roots left in the body politic to spread its hideous disease again. Make an effective job of it once for all. We want no chance, under the cloak of peace, for the return of this monster.

"The time has come to conquer or submit," wrote President Wilson shortly after our declaration of war. It is true. Can any one doubt what would have happened to the United States of America if Prussian autocracy had dictated terms of peace to vanquished Allies and as part of those terms had taken over the allied fleet and obtained territory in Canada? Or can any one doubt what will now happen to all the democracies if the present Pan-Germany, now existing by means of Prussian victories in this war, is during the next ten years consolidated, organized, Prussianized—and then, a fighting machine twice as powerful as the machine of 1914, hurled against the democracies? With an army of seven or eight million men trained to the hour, with equipped reserves of ten or twelve million more, with a complete network of military railroads capable of concentrating the units of this engine of destruction wherever military strategy shall designate, and with aeroplanes and transatlantic submarines in proportion, what chance will the democracies have?

In the second place, it ought to be very clear that future power and prosperity on the part of the plain people of Germany will be no bar to securing our rights, provided, however, that this power and prosperity is not owned and controlled by Prussian autocracy so that it can again be forced into a huge fighting machine to put the rest of the world in terror. The spirit of Lafayette, although its fight against such masters is eternal, will not lead in a war of conquest or annihilation against the German people.

"We have no quarrel with the German people," said the President of the United States in his message of April 2, 1917. "We have no feeling toward them but one of sympathy and friendship. It was not upon their impulse that their government acted in entering this war. It was not with their previous knowledge or approval. It was a war determined upon as wars used to be determined upon in the old, unhappy days when peoples were nowhere consulted by their rulers and wars were provoked and waged in the interest of dynasties or of little groups of ambitious men who were accustomed to use their fellowmen as pawns and tools." It was a war determined upon by the same Menace that thrust the democrat Lafayette into a dungeon, and which so hated democracy that when compelled to release him it attempted to impose terms that he should be deported to America, never again to place foot on Prussian or Austrian soil.

The corollary of this is that the best security for the rights of democracy is the establishment of a republic in Germany. A real republic, not a sham one. This is the one definite, concrete fact which would make the world safer for its peoples.

When will the German people see the light? When will there be a government of the people of Germany, for the people, and by the people? The shades of her dead, led to the slaughter by a merciless and heartless autocracy in a needless war, cry out for it. What say you, you men of Germany? Among you are men whose souls are brave and strong and true, an unnumbered host. How long, slaves, will you bend your backs to the lash of your military masters? They lied to you and made you believe the Fatherland was attacked, and led you, dupes, into a war of conquest. Your modern Pilate, in his blasphemous pride, with the name of God upon his lips and the blood of innocents upon his hands, is now crucifying Freedom upon his cross of iron. But the day of the resurrection will come; and how will your record stand then? Awake, ye free of Germany! When shall you come into your own?

Every hour that the coming of such a republic is shortened means just so much less agony for the peoples of the world. There is no better pledge for the safety of democracy. "Self-governed nations," said the President of the United States in the message referred to above, "do not fill their neighbour states with spies or set the course of intrigue to bring about some critical posture of affairs which will give them an opportunity to strike and make conquest. Such designs can be successfully worked out only under cover and where no one has the right to ask questions. Cunningly contrived plans of deception or aggression, carried, it may be, from generation to generation, can be worked out and kept from the light only within the privacy of courts or behind the carefully guarded confidences of a narrow and privileged class. They are happily impossible where public opinion commands and insists upon full information concerning all the nation's affairs."

XV

WHAT else? The union. The final act in the world-wide drama of democracy. The union of the democracies of the world to insure mutual protection and peace. I mean a union for this purpose of all those governments where the people, by their representatives, control. The union on two hemispheres of what the spirit of Lafayette foresaw, symbolized, and battled for on both.

The union ought to include the Austrian and German people themselves. It can never, however, include the Prussian military autocracy or any other military autocracy. I quote again from the President's message: "A steadfast concert for peace can never be maintained except by a partnership of democratic nations. No autocratic government could be trusted to keep faith within it or observe its covenants. It must be a league of honour, a partnership of opinion. Intrigue would eat its vitals away; the plottings of inner circles who could plan what they would and render account to no one would be a corruption seated at its very heart. Only free peoples can hold their purpose and their honour steady to a common end and prefer the interests of mankind to any narrow interest of their own.... One of the things that has served to convince us that the Prussian autocracy was not and could never be our friend is that from the very outset of the present war it has filled our unsuspecting communities and even our offices of government with spies, and set criminal intrigues everywhere afoot against our national unity of counsel, our peace within and without, our industries, and our commerce. Indeed it is now evident that its spies were here even before the war began; and it is unhappily not a matter of conjecture, but a fact proved in our courts of justice, that the intrigues which have more than once come perilously near to disturbing the peace and dislocating the industries of the country have been carried on at the instigation, with the support, and even under the personal direction of official agents of the Imperial Government accredited to the Government of the United States."

The union must be a union to keep the future safe against war, a league to compel every nation after the close of the present war to settle any claim it may have against its neighbour in the same way that individuals settle their disputes—by rules of right and reason instead of by the law of might. It must be "some definite concert of power that will make it virtually impossible that any such catastrophe should ever overwhelm us again." In a memorable address to the Senate of the United States on January 22, 1917, the President urged that the United States enter into such a league after the close of the present war, and on the point of effectiveness said: "Mere agreements may not make peace secure. It will be absolutely necessary that a force be created, as a guarantor of the permanency of the settlement, so much greater than the force of any nation now engaged or any alliance hitherto formed or projected, that no nation, no probable combination of nations, could face or withstand it. If the peace presently to be made is to endure it must be a peace made secure by the organized major force of mankind."

XVI

"*Cur non?*"—"Why not?" The union of the democracies will be the culmination of the world-wide drama begun by the spirit of Lafayette.

Jesus Christ, nineteen hundred years ago in his Sermon on the Mount, said to the wondering multitude: "For verily I say unto you, till heaven and earth pass, one jot or one tittle shall in no wise pass from the law, till all be fulfilled." Since then, as sure and certain as the evolution of time itself, the evolution of the law has been toward such a union.

"God's ways seem dark, but soon or late
They touch the shining hills of day;
The evil cannot brook delay,
The good can well afford to wait.
Give ermined kings their hour of crime,
Ye have the future grand and great
The safe appeal of truth to time."

Year has followed year and century has followed century, and through it all, surely, slowly, often torn and twisted out of shape but always growing, evolving, moving onward, the law has followed the safe appeal of truth to time, toward this great goal. One jot or one tittle shall in no wise pass from it till all be fulfilled. It is the spirit of Lafayette that leads. It was he who saw "the glory of the coming of the Lord." He saw fulfilled in fact the union of the separate democracies on one hemisphere; his spirit sees the vision of their union on two.

Gaze for a moment on what this soldier spirit has looked down upon in the past and on the vision of what it sees for the future.

Centuries ago individual man settled all his disputes with individual man by fighting. It was the primitive method. There was no law: might made right. The spirit saw savage primeval force, unconquered, untaught, powerful and brutal in the wanton exercise of its strength.

Then, under the safe appeal of truth to time, there gradually evolved, as between man and man, the method of voluntary submission to a judicial tribunal. Twisted and gnarled was this growth however, for even under Anglo-Saxon law the right of trial by battle was jealously guarded, and lasted for many years. A noble knight charged with an offense could always demand trial by battle; and if he succeeded in running through the body or otherwise disabling the man who made the accusation, he thereby established his own innocence and was acquitted by the court. This also the spirit saw.

Then gradually force was conquered, tamed, and used; and there evolved the modern court backed by the harnessed force of the community—backed by force sufficient to compel individual man to settle his disputes in court instead of by fighting, and if he refused and chose to fight, sufficient to compel him to desist and to punish him for his attempt. Force, a human Niagara, wild from the beginning, now controlled and directed by a higher law. Imagine the modern courts of our cities and states without the backing of organized force—courts and judges and rules of judicial procedure with no force to support them, and each individual in the community vested with the option in case of a dispute with a neighbour to settle that dispute by attacking the neighbour! We should have anarchy within six months.

What about nations? What has the spirit seen there? For nations are merely large collections of individuals. The same law of evolution governs both.

The first and primitive method of settling disputes between nations, and for a long time the only one, was war; and this the spirit beheld. Then gradually evolved the method of voluntary submission to a judicial tribunal such as the tribunal now existing at The Hague, each nation retaining, however, its right of trial by battle. The next method, the vision of the future, the new internationalism of which the living Lafayette was the symbol, is the harnessing of the united force of the peoples of the world, the union of the democracies to enforce the peace of the world. It is a vision of the union to form a modern court backed by force trained to obey the higher law, backed by force sufficient to compel nations to settle their disputes in court instead of by fighting. It is a vision of the war ogre, who has for centuries ravaged the world, at last shackled and bound; of the monster who with bloody claws and fangs has torn, ripped, and murdered his victims by the million, at last overcome; a vision of this evil brute of war conquered, and of primeval force trained, civilized, and forging the chains to hold this devil of hell.

XVII

DID that Indian warrior who met Lafayette in the American wilderness speak more wisely than he knew? Were the footsteps of this soldier of France directed by the Great Spirit? Who can tell!

This must be the last war. We shall not hand down to our children this heritage of calamity. Our Revolutionary War settled for all time the independence of these United States of America. The Civil War settled for all time the question of slavery in this hemisphere. This war must and shall settle for all time the question of military autocratic domination of the world. "The time has come to conquer or submit."

And if after we have checked and curbed this natural foe to liberty there shall arise a concert of the powers of the world, a world-wide union to insure and enforce future peace, a union based not merely on treaty obligations which may be avoided, or on a contract which may be broken, but on a wide understanding and realization that organized democracy must in the future act concertedly as the police of the world—then by just so much as we make posterity safe, the awful sacrifice will not have been made in vain.

We build for posterity. "*Cur non?*"—"Why not?" It is the spirit of Lafayette that calls. And with the call we hear from the heavens the chant of a mighty chorus, singing not the hymn of hate but the pæan of peace on earth, good-will toward men.

Those who do not know us gibe at us and throw our sins in our teeth. But this mightiest of democracies is at last awakening, is casting out the evil genii of opulence, is girding on its sword for the great work. Soldier of freedom, thou camest to us in the time of our greatest need. "Now," thou saidst, "is precisely the moment to serve your cause." Symbol of the united democracies of the world, symbol of a union which will make the earth safe for its peoples, symbol of a union of peace, we are led by thy spirit. We fight for democracy; we build for posterity.

And the rain descended, and the floods came, and the winds blew, and beat upon that house; and it fell not; for it was founded upon a rock.